ARMOUR BEARERS

*An Insider's Approach To The
Work of Protocol Officials
In A Church*

By

MIKE OLOROGUN

All scriptures quotations, unless otherwise indicated, are taken from the *New King James Version* of the Bible.

Scripture quotation marked KJV are taken from the *King James Version* of the holy bible.

Everywhere the amplified version (AMP) is used, note that it is the classical version.

ARMOUR BEARERS
An Insider's Approach To The
Work of Protocol Officials
In A Church

Contents

FOREWORD

Our God is a God of plan and purpose and from the nature around us, we can say without any iota of doubt that He also is a God of order. From the very first day in the Garden of Eden, Jehovah God began to exemplify this attribute of His.

Even after the fall of man, a God known for orderliness and purpose, had a plan for man and that plan followed a process and until the Christ came to fulfil God's plan, everything followed an order and process.

If this be the nature of our God, then it is incumbent on us to walk in His footstep – do things orderly. Whether the size of a ministry is small or big, God demands that things be done decently and in order.

The subject of Church Protocol as described in this mini-book by Pastor Mike Olorogun is the solution to one of the gaps in the way we handle God's servants among the churches.

The work of a Protocol officer is as tasking as they come. Each minister is anointed for a particular assignment by God. It is therefore notable that they are, each one of them, a peculiar person and therefore demands an equally peculiar treatment.

And therein lies the duty of the Protocol Officer to make conscious efforts to relate with these persons and make their assignment a lot more easier. We identified this need quite early in our ministry and sought the face of the Lord and how best to go about it and He gave us direction to create a Protocol Department. We obeyed and He gave a Pastor Mike Olorogun to lead this novel idea at the time.

Finding the right person for every assignment is as important as the assignment itself. Identifying willing persons to coordinate any ministry of help, for those who have some experience to share, could be challenging.

Pastor Mike Olorogun was not only available for the assignment, he was also willing. He embraced the task with the zeal only a few people could muster. He was ready to learn and find the men and women with whom to carry out the assignment.

He made work of conducting those extensive programs all year round less difficult and made our numerous guests feel at home while they were away from home.

Years have passed by, since we started the Protocol Department and most of those who pioneered the department have moved on to higher assignments in our ministry as Centre Pastors or have become General Overseers of their own ministries.

Magnanimously, Pastor Mike has found time from his busy schedule to put together this book to remind the Church of how to manage servants of God while they are on assignment for the Lord.

This book is a reminder to us of the importance of every arm of a ministry. Imagine what a chaotic scene it would be if there are no protocol officers to conduct the minister of the gospel. How more tedious his or her assignment would degenerate without the assistance of the protocol team members.

This book therefore is one of the answers to some of the issues in church management. I encourage every church worker to avail himself or herself a copy, if they ever want to serve the Lord better.

I am proud that this is coming just at the right time when the church needs the experience and knowledge of its older members.

Reverend Dr. Chris Tunde JODA

ACKNOWLEDGEMENT

Whatever I may have accomplished in the period I served as coordinator/pioneer head of the Protocol Department of one of Nigeria's leading Pentecostal Churches, I give all the credit to God who gave me the grace to do what I could not do in my power.

The encouragement to start and the confident assurance that the Lord was in this with me came from the leadership, vision and mentorship of the Pastor of Pastors, Reverend Dr. Chris Tunde Joda. It was a rare privilege for which I am eternally grateful.

I must not also forget to mention the immeasurable support I was privileged to enjoy from my pastor's wife and co-founder, Reverend (Mrs.) Victoria Ebun Joda.

Starting off on a path that has not been charted before can be daunting. I overcame any doubt and obstacles on the way because I had people who were willing to take the plunge with me. One of such persons is Pastor Sonny Williamson, a beloved brother and fellow servant in the Lord's service. Pastor Sonny was a staff of the ministry while I was not. I celebrate your dedication, reliability and total commitment to the assignment.

To my family which has continued to tolerate me when I devote my 'everything' in the service of the Lord, I am eternally grateful for your understanding.

Writing this mini-book was not my original intention. My original mandate was to return to where I left off with the Protocol Department when I moved to the United Kingdom, and train successors. I did that and left a seemingly training manual of a few pages. However, one man insisted the manual was not enough. A book of a sort, he insisted would do.

That man is the ever youthful pastor of Christ Chapel International Churches, Amuwo Odofin (International Headquarters) Niyi Olatunji, a utilitarian who remains an inspiration to me. Niyi, you persuaded me to do this, I am happy our path ever crossed.

After that initial foray, overcoming the teething problems of a new department included getting new members to join in making life more meaningful to visiting ministers, several young men and ladies yielded themselves for use. They are numerous to mention especially, as they continue to increase in number as the guest list also increases with time.

When I look back now, all I can say is, only the Lord can reward you ALL for your continued labour of love.

INTRODUCTION

My journey into what today has become a critical department in most churches across Nigeria and beyond, started in 1989. Simply identified then as the Protocol Department, it arose out of critical necessity at the time in the ministry which I belong. Voice of Faith Ministries a.k.a Christ Chapel International Churches (CCIC) was founded by one of the finest gifts of God to distraught mankind, a gentleman who, fresh from medical college wore the toga of the illimitable love of Christ as a second skin, far above the stethoscope which hung around his neck. He is Reverend Dr. Chris Tunde Joda.

This astute man of God in the early 1980s introduced to the Nigerian public what was then an uncommon way of worshipping God. It was one that simply said: come just the way you are. And just an experience in God's presence with an ecclesiastic praise and worship was all that you need to embrace God's unmerited favour to humanity. Through the gospel of faith and his undiluted teaching of the word of faith, many young and old persons thronged every of the services of Christ Chapel International Churches. It was not long that the world outside Lagos and Nigeria noticed this transformational message of God's grace and ministers of the gospel came in droves from the United States of America, Caribbean, The United Kingdom, and South Africa to Lagos following the trail of the voice of faith.

As the numbers of ministers increased yearly, it also required some measure of special attention be paid to these men and women of the word. For the young ministry at the time, keeping pace with these high profile ministers was an obvious challenge both in terms of human and material resources. But, most important was attending to them in such a way that they will feel at home while away from home, and enjoy their stay in Nigeria while it lasts.

This formed the background to what this mini-book is all about. During the years that will follow from 1989 unto the early 2000s, it was one awesome experience after another for me and the men and a few women who functioned as the Church's Protocol team. Leading ministers like Apostle Fredrick K.C. Price, Dr. Morris Cerrullo, Oral Roberts and his son Richard Roberts, Creflo Dollar Jnr, Benny Hinn, Christie Moore, Rhona May, etc. And from Nigeria the likes of Arch-Bishop Benson Idahosa (of blessed memory), Bishop Francis Wale Oke, Bishop David Oyedepo, Bishop Mike Okonkwo, Matthew Ashimolowo, and the list appears endless. These high profile ministers of the gospel with their entourage were all for our keeps during their days at the annual CCIC Camp Meeting. This usually runs for days and the task of accompanying, waking and sleeping around these anointed men of God was enough to transform the most implacable human.

Time moves fast and while I was enjoying this task, there was my circular work engagement to attend to aside from family. I woke up one morning to realize that it was retirement day for me. Many questions ran through my mind. Most of the questions I had no immediate answer to but, one thing became clear, and it was that the time to move on to a new environment had come. I left Nigeria but continued to serve in the Lord's vineyard.

Years have gone by since I left the shores of Nigeria. And each of these years have seen people accuse me of not preparing a proper successor to head the protocol department when I left Nigeria and migrated to the United Kingdom.

Unfortunately, this accusation is not exactly correct. The exigency of my relocation and God's elevation in my life, made some of those changes imperative. As a former head of Protocol and now a recipient of protocol services, I have come to see the need to gather a few of my thoughts and experience into a document. Especially the unimpressive conducts of some protocol teams and their members in recent time leaves a sour taste in my mouth.

I see a clear departure from the original purpose and intent of the man who led me into it. In an attempt to respond to the idea that there was 'abandonment' on my part, and correct some of the laxities that abound in some ongoing practices among workers in this very important department in a ministry, I have made a bold attempt to put out this guide book. It is my hope that this will serve as a guideline on what is expected from the leaders and members of the Protocol Department in a typical church; a support base towards fulfilling the ministry of those who have been called as part of the Protocol Department; and much more than these, it is hoped that operators will make the necessary adjustments, going forward.

I make bold to say that as a recipient of the instruction and vision of a protocol department, I am grateful to God for that privilege and the grace to function in that capacity. This is also a tribute to those men and women who worked with me during those days which I refer to as formative years of the department.

So, with the support of Rev. Dr. Chris Tunde Joda, we formed what can undeniably be described as the first protocol department which other Churches learnt from.

It is nearly 30 years since I got that mandate to establish and supervise a Protocol Department in the church. I have observed the work of a typical church protocol person grow in leaps and bounds. Yet, the number of unresolved issues emanating from the conducts of these men and women multiplies.

Perhaps, in resolving the gap that now exists between what it was and what it is now, the purpose for establishing a protocol department in any church must be laid bare right from the beginning. After all, it is a popular maxim that, "when the purpose of a thing is not known, abuse is inevitable."

That is why this book is about how it was then, what it is now and (or) what it should be.

Indeed, to all who labour in the Lord's vineyard to make the work of ministers easy, I salute your courage, zeal and love.

Chapter 1

IN THE BEGINNING

Why Protocol?

As I had stated earlier in the introduction to this book, church growth comes with its attendant demand on the human and material resources of the ministry. It is in the subconscious mind of those who carry the mandate to establish a ministry that addition to the size of the congregation is one of the evidence of the presence of God. I am yet to see however, any true servant of God who anticipated the actual dimension of growth the way the Lord multiplies. After all, He is the Lord of the harvest.

The experience that brought about the establishment of a department in charge of Protocol in Christ Chapel was in this wise. And I am sure a similar story can be said about churches who experienced and continue to experience growth.

For the ministry founded by Reverend Chris Tunde Joda and his wife, Reverend (Mrs.) Ebun Joda, this expansion came quite fast in the 1980s. At this time, most ministries were still grappling with the apathy in the society about this new wave of Christianity. It was phenomenal for the Jodas and the faith message handed to them.

The high volume of particularly international guest ministers visiting the Church especially during its annual Camp Meeting necessitated that certain special services be introduced to be provided for these growing number of foreign ministers and their Nigerian counterparts. Thus, arrangements such as:

a. Reception at the airport on arrival and seeing off during departure. This service is for both foreign and Nigerian resident ministers.
b. Transport throughout the duration of guest ministers stay with the church.
c. Provision of suitable accommodation for guests throughout their stay.
d. Feeding with strict consideration of the diversity of culture and tastes, etc.
e. Sight-seeing especially for foreign guests on days when they are not ministering.
f. Shopping for foreign guests and some form of recreation, as their schedule may permit.
g. Any other need that may arise in the course of the programme, among others.

It was in the midst of this expansive release of virtue from different ministers that the vision for the establishment of a Protocol Department was born. Its ultimate motive remains that of excellent service to others. This essential duty is found in Hebrews 13:2 (AMP).

"Do not forget or neglect or refuse to extend hospitality to strangers [in the brotherhood—being friendly, cordial, and gracious, sharing the comforts of your home and doing

your part generously], for through it some have entertained angels without knowing it".

The term protocol is derived from the Greek word *protokollon* a combination of two words: *protos* (first) *and kolla* (glue) combined to mean "the first glue". In contemporary usage however, protocol is likened to the glue which holds official life in the society together.

Protocol is defined as the system of rules and acceptable behaviour used at official ceremonies and occasions or a code of ceremonial forms and courtesies of procedures accepted as proper and correct in official dealing.

Starting the Department

Suffice to say that the Protocol Department is an arm of the ministry of helps. It therefore must function in line with the objective of giving service with the spirit of excellence and carrying out all its assignment as unto the Lord.

It was essentially the primary responsibility of this department to provide a hospitable and conducive environment for visiting guest ministers before, during and until the very last seconds of the departure of guests.

It is necessary to say at this point that the job is very rewarding and at the same time a 'thankless' job which comes with very demanding sacrifices.

In discussing the functions of a Protocol department, my cue is taken from the relationship that existed between

Prophet Elijah and his protégé, Elisha in the books of first and second Kings. Indeed, I will encourage anyone who wants to do a good job of protocol duties to study especially the character of Elisha as a servant of Elijah.

The protocol department at inception was saddled with the responsibility of:

- Guest reception and departure (both international and local).
- Visit and inspect usable hotels in a pre-determined geographical area and based on the findings, advice officials in the Church office who were responsible for hotel bookings.
- Organize vehicles, drivers and protocol personnel for the guest ministers, including their entourage.
- Oversee movement of guests from point A to B and maintain liaison with my protocol staff and the Church office. Making sure that guests depart from their hotels and arrive at meetings on time bearing in mind and putting into consideration traffic situation on the road depending on the intended destination. Of course, paramount to all of this, is the safety and security personnel and property.

For effective delivery as Head of the Protocol Department, it is essential that this person have unfettered access to the most senior pastor(s). This way, instructions will be clear and all ambiguity that may arise from third party interference are completely removed. Perhaps this access to the senior pastor, more than any other thing formed the secret to my success in building a meaningful Protocol Department.

And this is in strict line with the Elijah/Elisha principle that I talked about.

In this arrangement, it became important that I know what the set man wanted in order for me to function and achieve clearly defined mandates.

- With this knowledge, I constantly reminded myself that the guests were his. That they came at his invitation.

- It was also necessary that I worked hard to ensure that the mood and appearance of Protocol Members were cheerful and resonated gladness, at all times. After all, they are representatives of the Church of Christ.

- Another critical factor for anyone who must lead a Protocol Department is accountability. Like any leader, the head of the Protocol Department must be responsibility for the actions of members of his/her team. While genuine efforts must be made to minimize mistakes, but whenever it occurs, you must be ready to step in and take charge. The bulk must stop at someone's table.

Since I was working on the Elijah/Elisha model, I imagine that Elisha must have been very close to his master, Elijah. He must have had the privilege of sharing food, drink and other things with his master. He saw Elijah call forth fire from heaven twice:

1 kings 18:37-38
Hear me, O Lord, hear me, that this people may know that thou art the Lord God, and that thou hast turned their heart back again. Then the fire of the Lord fell, and consumed the burnt sacrifice, and the wood, and the stones, and the dust, and licked up the water that was in the trench.

Also in **2 Kings Chapter 1** Elijah called down fire from heaven twice to consume the captain and the 50 men - *...let fire come down from heaven and consume thee and thy fifty. And the fire of God came down from heaven, and consumed him and his fifty* (verses 10 and 12).

It is important to note that in this assignment, I was not my pastor's personal protocol person but head of the protocol department. That offered me very rare privilege of being close at different times and at different places with him and his ways of operation.

I had a very unique relationship with the servant of God, similar to the type Elijah and Elisha had. I witnessed him when he was not happy with things, when he was happy, under pressure and when he was in a relaxed mood. And when ministry assignments took us out of Lagos, I doubled as his Personal Protocol and Personal Assistant. Indeed, I had the privilege of sharing food and drinks with him.

From my study of the relationship between Elijah and Elisha, at no time was Elisha referred to as Elijah's friend.

With this knowledge, deliberately and consciously, I constantly reminded myself that my Pastor was not my friend and it was very necessary that I avoid the growth of familiarity with God's servant.

And even much greater burden on me was the realization that this anointed man of God was relying on me to function optimally hence, how I handle my duty was important to him. On his part, this great leader of men ensured that I understood what was required of me and his instructions were clear and precise.

Confronted with these realities, I remain in check at all times. "The fear of failure or disappointment marked the beginning of wisdom for me," and that spelt commitment.

I made sure that I was proactive. Always making sure that I knew what was required of me at all time. Also making suggestions and presenting plans ahead of every event.

For me on this assignment, I created no room for excuses because as someone rightly said, "Excuses don't exist, we make them."

To help me function appropriately and remain on top of my game, I made myself teachable and consciously worked at avoiding areas of potential friction through my actions.

For most servants of God, punctuality is not a subject for compromise. Having this at the back of my mind, I made sure I arrived on time and remotely, I influenced the punctuality of my team members.

It is equally necessary to point out that at the time which I write about, the Nigerian people did not have the present luxury of the mobile phones. Thus, achieving this was quite a task.

Making cohesiveness amongst team members was my priority. First, I made sure that I understood the job at hand. Then I went ahead to ensure that members of my team equally understood what was expected of us.

To crown this aspect of my conduct as a leader, I took responsibility for actions of my team members and apologized on their behalf, whenever mistakes were made.

To succeed in this onerous task, I constantly prayed with the team each morning especially during the annual Camp Meeting when the team is at its largest and volume of work is highest.

As the team leader, in a way of ensuring effective operational control and monitoring, I deliberately did not take up the function of driving any of the pool cars for guests or being attached to any particular guest.

Keeping within the rules is important if you must succeed. The Bible states in **1 Corinthians 14:40** - *Let all things be done decently and in order.* Unknown to many people, this is a weighty statement that must not be taken for granted.

John 2:14-16

And found in the temple those that sold oxen and sheep and doves, and the changers of money sitting:
And when he had made a scourge of small cords, he drove them all out of the temple, and the sheep, and the oxen; and poured out the changers' money, and overthrew the tables;
And said unto them that sold doves, Take these things hence; make not my Father's house a house of merchandise.

If a church is to operate in a decent and orderly fashion, there must be an authority over the house; the Pastor, Bishop, an Overseer, etc. This person has been chosen by God to provide vision, knowledge, understanding, sound doctrine, discipline and order.

Looking at **Acts 6:1-7,**
And in those days, when the number of the disciples was multiplied, there arose a murmuring of the Grecians against the Hebrews, because their widows were neglected in the daily ministration.
Then the twelve called the multitude of the disciples unto them, and said, It is not reason that we should leave the word of God, and serve tables.
Wherefore, brethren, look ye out among you seven men of honest report, full of the Holy Ghost and wisdom, whom we may appoint over this business.
But we will give ourselves continually to prayer, and to the ministry of the word.
And the saying pleased the whole multitude: and they chose Stephen, a man full of faith and of the Holy Ghost,

and Philip, and Prochorus, and Nicanor, and Timon, and Parmenas, and Nicolas a proselyte of Antioch:
Whom they set before the apostles: and when they had prayed, they laid their hands on them.
And the word of God increased; and the number of the disciples multiplied in Jerusalem greatly; and a great company of the priests were obedient to the faith.

The Bible never hides the human weaknesses of those who serve the Lord. The people were upset, talking, and complaining about what they saw going on. This sounds like life in many churches and organizations, today. It is important to study and understand how the apostles handled this problem. Five principles in these verses will form the basis of order in the church:

1. Effectiveness - The apostles knew their purpose and functioned in it.

2. Excellence - The apostles set a high goal of devoting themselves to prayer and the word.

3. Efficiency - The apostles realized a great harvest of people because they were efficient in their use of time and resources.

4. Organization - The apostles increased their level of organization to meet the needs of the people.

5. Faith – Without faith, I dare say that it is impossible for anyone to serve effectively and unto all-pleasing

to God without faith. It is clearly stated in **Hebrews 11:6**, *But without faith it is impossible to please Him (God)…*

Something happened and this prompted the change which made the church function better. Those who were subsequently appointed ministered to the widows in the power of the Holy Spirit. And the consequence was that those who gave themselves to the word and prayer, did so with excellence.

The result from this improvement in organization was quite glaring. The number of disciples increased greatly, and the whole project became more efficient. As they walked in faith, the apostles created an organization that was remarkable for its effectiveness, excellence, and efficiency.

Vision

Even though time, needs and operations has changed due to growth in size and scope of ministry, the original vision for the Protocol department has not changed. The Protocol department remains a ministry of service and the vision of the Protocol Department is based on service to others and this is found in **Hebrews 13:2** (NIV), *Show Hospitality to Strangers*.

Considering this demand of extending hospitality to strangers, as we daily carry out our functions as members of the protocol department, the mood and appearance of members must at all times exude cheerfulness, confidence and gladness of heart since, the Protocol Members are representatives of the church.

Purpose

Protocol Members are like the 'Special Services' section of the Church. Their particular area of focus is on the Pastorate and Guest Ministers. The impression which the Protocol Members make on guest ministers and the associates of guest ministers will greatly affect their perception of the Church. It is a common phrase in the corporate world that 'You don't have a second chance to make a first impression', this is also true for the church and in virtually every aspect of human endeavour.

In order to carry out this purpose of attending to the needs of the Pastorate and Guests of the ministry and leaving a lasting positive impression on them, some key activities are essential components of an ideal Protocol Department:

1. Preliminary engagement with guests prior to their scheduled arrival is not an issue that must be compromised. Establishing this preliminary engagement (either directly or indirectly through proxy, agents or via communication, etc.) with the guest to introduce the protocol and seek information on specific needs of the guest which needs to be taken care of during the visit is the first place to begin.

   What is there to know in this preliminary engagement?

a) Flight details and other logistic arrangements and components of journey instructions.
b) Preferred hotel or alternative accommodation arrangements.
c) Meals and special needs, where necessary.

This communication must be established in good time before scheduled arrival date and where for any reason this is not possible, such details must be provided as soon as possible on the day of guest' arrival.

2. Guest's hospitality prior to arrival. One other advantage in establishing preliminary contact with a guest is that the protocol team is able to liaise with relevant Airport Management services to provide a warm VIP reception for the guest. The protocol officers (at least two) should be at the Airport to receive the guest and present a 'Welcome Pack' to him or her.

a) The welcome pack can also be left in the hotel room prior to guest's arrival. The advantage the welcome pack confers on the ministry is that it helps to formally introduce the church to the guest as well as give key information about the church, location, immediate environment and city (profile).

b) In addition, a Pay-As-You-Go SIM Card Phone (loaded with reasonable credit) should be made available to a guest coming from a different country from your own, and it is made available at his/her hotel room. The reason for this is that most international guests would want to contact their families immediately on arrival.

Accommodation Arrangements

A suitable hotel should be arranged for the Guest Minister throughout the duration of the stay with the Church. The Guest Minister does not have to bother with making any arrangements for himself or herself. However, where an alternative arrangement is made such as in a situation where a brethren indicates interest to host the guest, the Protocol Team will liaise with the host (as required) to ensure that the guest is comfortably accommodated with all the relevant facilities provided.

From my experience over the years, this can be dodgy sometimes because even when the accommodation is suitable, some guests may not be comfortable staying with a host family. And if this decision to switch from the host family occurs mid-way into the guest's stay, it may become difficult to move such guest from the host's house for some obvious reasons.

For most guests needs, the chosen hotel or any accommodation for that matter, should have provisions where possible, for a visitor reception area as well as study area for the use of the guest minister, etc.

Provision of Refreshments

The Protocol Team liaises with the Guest Minister on his/her choice of menu (as applicable) and arranges catering services as may be required.

a)   It is advisable that the Team prepares in collaboration with other relevant departments/persons, a menu list of main items available in the hotel prior to the guest's arrival.

Local Transportation
The Protocol Team arranges local transportation for the Guest Minister. The transportation should usually be in a convoy and the following points are to be noted for this purpose:

a)   Ensure that all drivers in the convoy understand the speed limits and routes for conveying the Guest Minister.
b)   All drivers must obey or abide by local traffic rules to avoid confrontation with local traffic control authorities.
A meeting is usually held prior to guest's arrival to agree on the Journey Management Plan (JMP) which comprises drawings of approved routes and speed limits.
c)   All drivers shall strictly comply with this plan throughout the duration of Guest's visit.
d)   The lead driver shall maintain agreed speed limits and remain in convoy always.

Guest's Shopping and Sight-seeing
The Protocol Team is responsible for arrangement of escorts for Guest Ministers while shopping and sight-seeing (if required). Information on available shopping malls should be included in the provided welcome pack.

Core Values of the Protocol Department

The Protocol Department must be guided by certain core values which every of its member should demonstrate. Every Protocol Member should be:

a)   SPIRITUAL

Since we understand that the physical is controlled by the spiritual, the Protocol Department members take their spiritual lives, especially prayers and study of the word very seriously. **John 6:63** (NKJV), *It is the Spirit that gives life, the flesh profits nothing.*

b)   POLITE AND CHEERFUL

As it is essential that protocol officials interact with people from different backgrounds, the members will always maintain a polite and cheerful appearance at all times.

c)   ORGANISED

As a department saddled with the organization of the travels, accommodation and other related matters of Guest Ministers, each member is expected to demonstrate a high level of organization and this must be visible in their individual lives, as well.

d)   SUBMISSIVE

Ordinarily as a believer, we are mandated to submit to each other. First to the church leadership and then the Guest Ministers and this is to be done out of respect for God. This is in spite of the fact that certain aspects of the assignment may appear complicated and quite tasking. The conduct of the protocol official must at all times be guided by **Eph. 5:21,** *Submitting yourselves one to another in the fear of God.*

e)   EXCELLENCE

For everyone who serves as a Protocol Member, he or she should be committed to efficiency and excellence. That person must always seek for ways to improve himself or herself, because the God we serve is a God of excellence.

f)   PATIENCE

One virtue that must be imbibed by an average Protocol Member is patience. To serve in this position, that person must be committed to exhibiting patience at all times bearing in mind that people are coming to the Lord with their burdens and their burdens are diverse.

Gal 5:22-23 *But the fruit of the [Holy] Spirit [the work which His presence within accomplishes] is love, joy (gladness), peace, patience (an even temper, forbearance), kindness, goodness (benevolence), faithfulness, 23 Gentleness (meekness, humility), self-control (self-restraint, continence). Against such things there is no law [that can bring a charge].*

g)   PUNCTUALITY & TIMELINESS

This attribute is one of the most important and where it is not made a part of the individual Protocol Member's lifestyle, it could be a barrier to fulfilling the overall objective of the ministry.

Colossians 4:5 (AMP), *Behave yourselves wisely [living prudently and with discretion] in your relations with those of* *the outside world (the non-Christians), making the very most of the time and seizing (buying up) the opportunity.*

Expectations

Naturally speaking, people build expectations based on what is told them of the objective of a thing. Similarly, there are expectations from the person serving as a protocol official based often on the literal understanding people have from mere mention of the name.

A few of these expectations can only be met when members of the department manifest the following attributes:

1. Spiritual Responsibility
All members in the Protocol Department are expected to maintain a high level of spirituality at all times to enable them effectively serve the ministers of God. Therefore, each Protocol Department member is expected to spend quality time praying and studying the Word of God – Joshua ministered unto Moses but he also looked into spiritual matters.

Exodus 24:12 – 13, *And the Lord said unto Moses, come up to me into the mount,… And Moses rose up, and his minister Joshua: and Moses went up into the mount of God.*

2. Elisha was also a minister to Elijah and eventually became a great man of God in Israel.

1 Kings 19:21, …*Then he (Elisha) arose, went after Elijah, and ministered unto him.*

3. A successful protocol official must be full of the Holy Ghost such that it shows in the level of excellence in his work.

Daniel 6:3, *Then this Daniel was preferred above the presidents and princes, because an excellent spirit was in him.*

The need to have a teachable spirit is an essential attribute if you must succeed as a protocol official. A willingness to learn at every opportunity ensures that you are not taken unaware by developments rather, you are ever ready to handle every assignment as it arises.

The Link

Interestingly, most times it is taken for granted the essential role of protocol to the Pastor and how it is connected with the people that are served. The assignment of the protocol department and its personnel is to serve as a LINK between the server and the served. This way, the server is freed from serving while the served is properly taken care of.

The chain of a ship anchor is the link between the ship and the anchor. The ship is relying on the chain (the link) to maintain its connection with the anchor. A ship at anchor does not see the anchor secured at the seabed neither does the anchor see the ship afloat but, the connection links the two. This connect is what the ship depends on while at anchor.

Protocol is the art of combining good manners and common sense to make effective communication possible.

Chapter 2

RESPONSIBILITY

Responsibility is central to every kingdom assignment. It is at the very center of how well we excel in every assignment. Have you found a man worthy of use to the Lord? He/she must eschew a responsible character. This important attribute in a life demands show of commitment and it entails keeping in good order whatever is trusted unto your hand.

There are different levels of responsibility required of a Protocol worker and this is ever increasing as the assignment increases. To function effectively and qualify as a responsible protocol official, three prerequisites are essential.

Spiritual
The kingdom of God is a Theocracy and not a Democracy. For this reason, every member of the protocol department, unit or by whatever name the ministry chooses to identify it, is expected to obey instructions given by the Pastorate and the leader of the department.

i.   Involvement in Church Activities:
Notice that it is recommended in **Heb.10:25**, *Not forsaking the assembling of ourselves together, as the manner of some is.*

Involvement in Church activities constitutes some of the best way to learn and be abreast of the direction the spirit is leading the church at a particular time.

ii.   Regular and Punctual for Workers' Meeting:
This helps to prepare the member for the day's assignment and most times, only regular and punctual members receive the vital information necessary for the needed assignment.

iii.   Regular and Punctual for Meetings of the Protocol Department.

iv.   Prayerfully preparing for any activity that he or she may be assigned to perform.

v.   Like a military personnel, individual protocol must be available for any tasks assigned during services and meetings.

vi.   Moreover, he or she must be committed to providing excellent service for any assigned tasks with the Protocol Department and church at large.

Self-Improvement

Every member of the Protocol department are expected to continually seek ways to improve themselves in the area of service at their duty post. While the church will provide opportunities for members to develop themselves, each individual member is also encouraged to take this personal. Therefore, each member is expected to:

i. Find out better ways of performing the duties of the Protocol department.

ii. Continue to seek faster and better ways of performing tasks for excellent service delivery.

iii. Attend seminars and programs that will assist in improving his or her skills and effectiveness in assigned areas.

Local Assembly

Another responsibility that is paramount to the Protocol member is that of abiding by the regulations of the Church to which he or she belongs, no matter how stringent this may sometimes appear. Accordingly, every member of the department is expected to be:

i. Subject to the authority of the Church. According to **Hebrews13:17,** *Obey them that have the rule over you, and submit yourselves: for they watch for your souls, as they that must give account, that they may do it with joy, and not with grief: for that is unprofitable for you.*

Chapter 3

ETHICS AND CONDUCT

There are minimum levels of acceptable behaviors expected from every member of the Protocol Department. These include but not limited to the following:

While Transporting A Guest Minister:

a) As a rule and this is also a critical security issue, protocol members shall ensure that the Guest Minister is not carried along with anybody else including friends, wife and children of the officiating protocol office. The only exception to this rule is at the express request of the Guest Minister concerned.

b) In the event of driving in a convoy, the convoy drivers shall always make sure that their cars are in close proximity to the lead car.

c) The head of the protocol team bears the responsibility for the after use parking and dispatch of the utilized vehicles.

d) Drivers shall put their mobile phones on silence mode throughout the period of commuting and driving a Guest Minister. It is important to note that drivers shall not make calls nor receive telephone calls while driving a Guest Minister.

e) Akin to stating the obvious is the fact that drivers shall always keep the vehicle conveying the Guest Minister and indeed every minister, clean and tidy at all times. No food leftover or any other dirt should be found in the car. For this reason, it is important that from the planning stage concerted effort should be taken to ensure as much as it is practicable, not to change cars or drivers at short notice because if it so happens, the replacement driver may not have adequate time to maintain the cleanliness of the car.

f) It is also the obligation of the driver to make sure that the Guest Minister's car is protected at all times.

g) Another demand is that drivers (protocol members) shall ensure that a Guest Minister's car interior maintains a comfortable temperature and this should be ready at least 20 minutes prior to take off, in all seasons.

h) In the event of an emergency, it may warrant that drivers be changed without prior notice and protocol members for such reasons should be prepared for such a time without expressing any displeasure.

i) A rule that must not be broken is that drivers shall not speak to a Guest Minister directly except in response to a question from the guest minister. In fact, only greetings are allowed and that is how stringent the assignment is.

Approaching Service Venue and During the Service:

a) Protocol Members shall ensure that nobody is allowed to touch a Guest Minister while ushering him or her to and from the altar. The passage way of a Guest Minister should be clear and unhindered by people.

b) It is mandatory that protocol members ensure that a Guest Minister is accompanied at all times while in church. He or she shall not be left alone in the designated reception area, at any time.

c) Like a soldier on assignment, an officiating protocol officer shall be on alert for a Guest Minister's call for support, always.

d) The leader of the protocol team must ensure that cars are fueled in good time to avoid vehicle running short of fuel while in use. It is not advisable that cars be sent for fueling while the guest is in Church during service since it is hard to predict the traffic situation on the road, and any likely queues at fuel stations, etc.

e) Just as it is with the law of the land, it is not permissible for any protocol driver to drive any vehicle without a valid driver's license.

f) As much as it is practicable, guests' vehicles should be parked together in a designated area.

Uniform and Identification:

a) For ease of identification, it is mandatory that members of the protocol team maintain uniformity in dress code.

b) The colors of the accessories such as ties and scarves shall be uniform for both male and female.

c) Members are expected to wear their name tags while officiating to make identification easy for the Guest Ministers.

d) Personal hygiene and appearance is the sole responsibility of every individual protocol member. Protocol officers work long hours and the weather in the tropics could be quite intense and this is capable of causing much sweating. With this at the back of our minds, care must be taken to maintain clean personal hygiene at all times.

e) Modesty is another prerequisite attribute of a protocol member. Just like every Christian is expected to display modesty in lifestyle, the protocol personnel are to do the same. Dressing in a sensually provocative manner produces inclinations to evil desires and must be discouraged.

Communication and Discipline

These two items constitute some of the most enduring value that must guide the conduct of members of a Protocol Team. There appears to be no substitute to these mannerism for any member called to this assignment.

a) Protocol staff must ensure that while they are in the car or with the guest, they do not speak in a language that the guest may not understand, such as pidgin and (or) vernacular.

b) It is another of the team leader's responsibility to ensure that the technical department makes available current and modern discrete wireless communication devices for members on duty.

c) Proper training on the use of these devices should also be provided.

d) Members of the team shall treat all information with confidentiality and shall not divulge details of a Guest Minister's itinerary to a third party.

e) Members are expected to exhibit high level of professionalism at all times.

f) Unavoidably, some form of relationship develops if a protocol officer had worked in the past with a guest minister. However, it must be noted that in spite of what could be described as a cordial past association, the guest is still 'not your friend' and every appearance of undue familiarity should be avoided.

Discipline

I believe that strict adherence to law and order is fundamental to doing exploits in life and ministry. It should therefore, be the practice in all areas of protocol operations.

1 Corinthians 9:25 (AMP), *Now every athlete who goes into training conducts himself temperately and restricts himself in all things. They do it to win a wreath that will* *soon wither, but we [do it to receive a crown of eternal blessedness] that cannot wither.*

Meetings:
An essential ingredient in any human association, meetings for members of a Protocol Team is akin to fish and water, that is their habitat. There should be different levels and timing for meetings in the Protocol Department.

It is important to understand that the Protocol Department is slightly different from other departments due to the peculiar services that it provides in the Church. They relate directly with the guests by virtue of their function. As a result, the meetings should be scheduled before every major event where a high number of guests are expected, such as Camp meetings/Conventions. Such meetings should be structured in such a way that it meets the objectives of the department.

Post Event
This is a meeting conducted after every hosting of a Guest Minister and the focus is to capture the lessons learnt. The things to be considered include:

a) Things that were done very well.
b) Things that can be improved upon.
c) The things that can be avoided or stopped outright, knowing that such is no longer required.

Monthly or Quarterly

This is an engagement session arranged primarily for performance review. The things to be considered may include:
a) Seek opportunities for continuous improvements.

b) Proffer strategies on way-forward.

c) Depending on the frequency of activities in the ministry, this meeting and the 'post event Meeting' may happen inside the same meeting.

d) There should be short time of exhortation and prayer during such meetings.

Chapter 4

TEAM AND SCHEDULES

Essence of the Roster

Roster or in some cases schedule for the protocol team is designed to ensure that you have enough officials to keep operations running smoothly without hitches.

This schedule or roster is expected to be created by the leader or anyone he or she deems competent enough to handle the assignment. It provides the team with an idea of who is working on what day, time of resumption and with which guest minister, etc.

Roster may be subject to change at short notice (what in business management system is referred to as on-call scheduling which requires that an official remain on stand-by and could be called up on short notice). This sudden changes that is allowed in roster management, are most times very necessary for the smooth running of a church program.

A situation where a protocol member does not know or is not sure of what to do next, unaware of which guest he or she is working with, should be avoided completely. It is for this reason that prayers and short meetings at the beginning of the day are very important.

Advantages of a Roster

a)   Unknown to many persons, a properly considered roster could make all the difference in the operation of the protocol department. And this is because the leader understands the strengths and weaknesses of his or her team members and in distributing them to guest ministers coming for the church's event, he or she considers what is known of the team members in scheduling them for each minister.

For instance, what a mismatch it would be to attach an extremely introverted protocol member to a minister with a reputation for chatting up his or her protocol officer during a ride. The most appropriate protocol officer for such a minister is a skilled communicator and someone knowledgeable about current national topics to sustain conversation with such a minister.

Similarly, the leader has the onerous task in identifying members of the team who are skilled in driving at night in the event that the programs end at nights and you need to navigate through the city traffic to get to the residence of the guest minister(s). It must be noted that it is not every driver, no matter how skilled can manage driving at night.

b)   A good roster will assist a great deal in the team making avoidable mistakes or even accidents, because it will help eliminate the incidence of exhaustion when you do not have enough hands on duty to handle the number of guests for a program.

It is easy to cite from the distance a disorganized protocol team which is not guided by a properly drawn up roster. Confusion could be worn as a cloth by ill-prepared protocol team.

c)   Furthermore, a schedule or roster will assist in knowing where your members' skills are lacking and assist in recommending further trainings to enhance their performance, etc.

d)   One of the most important advantages that a roster confers on your department is that it enables you (the leader) fill the most busy program schedule with your most experienced protocol team members.

Protocol and Other Departments

If roles and functions are properly understood in the way they ought to be, the protocol official could be likened to an orderly to an army general.

An orderly takes care and most times, is entrusted with the general's personal items. He is usually not a commissioned officer. He travels in the same car with his boss, the general. When the general arrives at a venue, all eyes are on the general and the orderly may not even be noticed but his presence and functions cannot be ignored or disregarded, because he is a member, although silent, of the general's entourage. In a lot of cases, he is the one holding the general's personal cell phone and may be, wallet. He has to be within easy reach of the general because of the personalized nature of his function.

It is noteworthy that the Protocol Department members can only execute their assignment with good results when they are adequately in sync with other related departments which the church may have.

Depending on the size, vision and structure of the church's administration, to better execute the purpose of the Protocol Department, the department must identify and remain in constant harmonic working relationship with some essential units or departments, at each of the church's program.

1. Security: The security person who protects the guest automatically protects the protocol team member as well.

2. Hospitality: This people takes care of the need of the guests and make arrangements for them where necessary. For instance, if the guest needs a drink, he would necessarily whisper to the protocol officer. Should he or she want to use the restroom, he or she will whisper to the protocol. It is now the duty of the protocol officer to relate with other service providers as required.

3. Ushering team: Ushering team should remember that they are silent members in managing guests and their entourage and this is included in their planning.

4. Leaders: There may be other leaders who may want to relate or interact with the guest, for seamless operation, they may have to approach the protocol officer for the avoidance of confusion. The guest

may tell or give certain instructions to the protocol officer such that other leaders may not be privy to.

5. Travel and Transport: this team coordinates the travel and transport and other related plans for Guest Ministers and members of their team.

6. Accommodation and Welfare: often, this department or unit handles the accommodation, feeding, shopping and other related matters of Guest Ministers and members of their entourage.

7. Guides and Guards: while the function of this group may appear similar to that of the protocol members, they are not exactly the same. The Guards and Guides stay with guest ministers during services and make sure that the crowd does not disturb the guests.

8. Other Services: by whatever name other teams may be called, they are those who are responsible for handling any other special services outside of those mentioned above.

Also, the pastor may pass certain information to the guest through the protocol officer such that other leaders may not be privy to. They are also able to pass information in trust from the guest to the leadership. Thus, the protocol team serve as an important link in the chain of affairs. Therefore, shoving aside and disrespecting the protocol officer most times connotes disrespect to the guest himself especially, if the guest gets to know of this or observe it while it took place.

Whenever it becomes necessary to send information to the guest from any member of the organizing team, it is usually advised that such instructions or information be passed through the head of the team irrespective of the staff working directly with the guests because, ideally, the leader of the team should be a more matured person. He is responsible and accountable to leadership for the actions of his team members.

This explains why it is necessary and very helpful for the head of the protocol team to be the one who introduces the protocol personnel to the guest on arrival and he or she should make himself or herself known to the guests as the leader of the group.

Changing a protocol officer attached to a minister without first informing the guest, is tantamount to disrespect of the guest. Caution must be taken in handling such aspect when it becomes necessary.

Notice also that a guest who has developed a closeness with the protocol officer may complain to such protocol officer of his or her displeasure on certain things which he or her may not tell the host pastor.

To my dismay, I have seen how often we tend to show respect to the guest yet utterly disrespect his closest ally for that period.

We attach protocol members to guests because of the belief that protocol is necessary for the services he or she stands to render to the guest, especially in seeing to the personal and immediate needs of the guest, and if that is the case, people should exercise caution while dealing with protocol staff especially those attached to guests.

The Apostle Paul said in the book of **1 Corinthians 12: 12-27,**

For just as the body is one and yet has many parts, and all the parts, though many, form [only] one body, so it is with Christ (the Messiah, the Anointed One).
For by [means of the personal agency of] one [Holy] Spirit we were all, whether Jews or Greeks, slaves or free, baptized [and by baptism united together] into one body, and all made to drink of one [Holy] Spirit.
For the body does not consist of one limb or organ but of many.
If the foot should say, Because I am not the hand, I do not belong to the body, would it be therefore not [a part] of the body?
If the ear should say, Because I am not the eye, I do not belong to the body, would it be therefore not [a part] of the body?
If the whole body were an eye, where [would be the sense of] hearing? If the whole body were an ear, where [would be the sense of] smell?
But as it is, God has placed and arranged the limbs and organs in the body, each [particular one] of them, just as He wished and saw fit and with the best adaptation.
But if [the whole] were all a single organ, where would the body be?
And now there are [certainly] many limbs and organs, but a single body.

And the eye is not able to say to the hand, I have no need of you, nor again the head to the feet, I have no need of you.

But instead, there is [absolute] necessity for the parts of the body that are considered the more weak.

And those [parts] of the body which we consider rather ignoble are [the very parts] which we invest with additional honor, and our unseemly parts and those unsuitable for exposure are treated with seemliness (modesty and decorum),

Which our more presentable parts do not require. But God has so adjusted (mingled, harmonized, and subtly proportioned the parts of) the whole body, giving the greater honor and richer endowment to the inferior parts which lack [apparent importance],

So that there should be no division or discord or lack of adaptation [of the parts of the body to each other], but the members all alike should have a mutual interest in and care for one another.

And if one member suffers, all the parts [share] the suffering; if one member is honored, all the members [share in] the enjoyment of it.

Now you [collectively] are Christ's body and [individually] you are members of it, each part severally and distinct [each with his own place and function].

This goes to support the notion that the function of protocol team members is not special or superior but by virtue of their closeness and nature of the personalized services that they render to guests, their function is deemed peculiar.

During that very short duration of their time with guests, they multi-task and function as armor bearer, personal assistant and protocol officer all rolled in one, in a twinkle of an eye.

It is for the inter relationship of the different units in a church that the popular saying, 'No man is an Island' is applicable. Success for the entire ministry is only accomplished when these different units play their parts effectively and efficiently.

Understanding the Role of Protocol

The role and position of the head of protocol should be given adequate recognition and respect in the ministry's hierarchy. This may appear like asking for preference but, this recognition becomes an essential 'endorsement' if that person is to enjoy the respect and cooperation of members of his or her team.

Given the depth of discipline required to function in the protocol department, an appearance of regimentation equally requires a measure of recognition for the occupier of such an office to have ample control over the team members.

While it can be stated without equivocation that the protocol team is not in any way more special than any other department, however, fact remains that these are men and women saddled with the responsibility of looking after guests on behalf of the Church.

It is essential therefore that instruction and information is communicated to the head of Protocol department since he is the link between the Pastorate and Leadership of the church, and the protocol team members. Again we must be reminded of the need for things to be done decently and in order (**1 Cor. 14:40**).

This stand about the headship of the Protocol department is sine qua non is that person is to fulfill the purpose of establishing the department. It is either he or she is in charge or is not. By-passing the head of protocol and passing instructions to his team members without his knowledge will tantamount to building a house of confusion and commotion.

Chapter 5

THE GEHAZI EXPERIENCE

Avoiding the Pitfall

Let no pretense be made that guest ministers are human beings and they mostly observe the sacrifices and long hours protocol members put in to attend to them and their needs. And from experience, most servants of the Lord are usually very appreciative and want to show their appreciation to these 'soldiers of the cross', after all they (ministers) are human. However, but it is advised that such offers to extend material appreciation MUST be respectfully declined.

Worse still, the protocol team members must avoid the temptation to ask for and (or) receive material or cash gifts from guest ministers. The protocol member must always have it at the back of his or her mind that no man can pay them for their services. Therefore, the focus must be to render service as unto the Lord.

The Bible gives us enough examples of how this works.

Elisha became a prophet after his master Elijah was taken up into heaven according to the word of the Lord in **1 Kings 19:16** (AMP), *And anoint Jehu son of Nimshi to be* *king over Israel, and anoint Elisha son of Shaphat of Abel-meholah to be prophet in your place.*

Subsequently, Gehazi became servant of Elisha when Elisha became the prophet in the place of his former master. Elisha was a man full of experience in servant-hood and very focused on his call to serve. He was determined that nothing would stand between him and his service to Elijah. He was persuaded that his service was as unto the Lord.

Three times Elisha said to Elijah, *As the Lord lives and as your soul lives, I will not leave you* (**2 Kings 2:2,4,6**).

Unfortunately, Gehazi's focus was on 'what is in it for me?' He was conscious of his personal gain. This is why it is strongly advised that members of the protocol team must avoid the temptation to ask for financial or material favour from guests. Unknown to many who work with guests, guests when they are alone talk. This may not necessarily mean that the guest will report the team member to his or her pastor or leader, but they sometimes engage in discussions about the good and the not so good conducts of protocol members, amongst themselves and may be, with your pastor too.

In my years as head of protocol department, I have painfully experienced incidences when guest ministers complained about protocol members seeking for financial favour from them to a pastor. Gehazi did not consider that his master Elisha would get to know of his behind the scene maneuvers.

Let us take a look at the story of Gehazi in **2 Kings 5:20-27**

But Gehazi, the servant of Elisha the man of God, said, Behold, my master spared this Naaman the Syrian, in not receiving from his hands what he brought. But as the Lord lives, I will run after him and get something from him.
So Gehazi followed after Naaman. When Naaman saw one running after him, he lighted down from the chariot to meet him and said, Is all well?
And he said, All is well. My master has sent me to say, There have just come to me from the hill country of Ephraim two young men of the sons of the prophets. I pray you, give them a talent of silver and two changes of garments.
And Naaman said, Be pleased to take two talents. And he urged him, and bound two talents of silver in two bags with two changes of garments and laid them upon two of his servants, and they bore them before Gehazi.
When he came to the hill, he took them from their hands and put them in the house; and he sent the men away, and they left.
He went in and stood before his master. Elisha said, Where have you been, Gehazi? He said, Your servant went nowhere.
Elisha said to him, Did not my spirit go with you when the man turned from his chariot to meet you? Was it a time to accept money, garments, olive orchards, vineyards, sheep, oxen, menservants, and maidservants?

Therefore the leprosy of Naaman shall cleave to you and to your offspring forever. And Gehazi went from his presence a leper as white as snow.

Lessons to Learn

Gehazi lacked integrity.

He was driven with greed.

He lied against his master.

He demanded and collected money and material gifts.

And in order to cover up for his first lie, he also lied to his master.

The consequence of this display of greed and not trusting the Lord to meet his needs, Gehazi and his offspring ended up with leprosy. Note that he did not suffer the consequences of his sins alone, the curse from the man of God affected his offspring as well. This calls for extreme caution on the part of those engaged to serve as protocol officers.

It is important for those who are called to serve in the Lord's vineyard that He is a God of plan and purpose. And He is a rewarder of them who diligently seek him. It is already a privilege to serve in any capacity in the Lord's vineyard and to those who serve diligently, at the appointed time, He rewards them in a way and manner which man cannot do.

Welfare

Should there be a special treatment for protocol officials? Is it not enough that there is the assurance of God blessing for those who serve Him diligently? If indeed there is a reason for special attention, what are the peculiar challenges that protocol members face that other ministries of help are not exposed to? Questions as these have over time arisen when demand for some special welfare arrangement for the protocol team is presented in churches. Suffice to say that this debate is mostly unnecessary.

Many persons have resisted proposals to make provisions of some welfare incentive to members of the protocol team just as a few others with an understanding of the peculiar nature of the assignment have argued in support of certain incentives for them.

Argument against:

1. Everybody in the Church is providing service as unto the Lord and therefore no one group or persons should be seen as more important than others.

2. Protocol members are servants of the Lord, they are no more special and should not be treated as such.

3. If we have to provide incentives for members of the Protocol team, we might as well provide incentives for the other groups.

4. Protocol members are not the only team working long hours.

5. All these are true and there may not be 'any special' argument to support the demand for certain incentive for the protocol team however, I have experience of the inner working of the protocol team and I believe unlike some people, I should know.

Argument for:

While in the eyes of the larger church there may be no significantly compelling reasons for advocating for some incentives for protocol staff, I do so for reason such as;

1. Protocol members spend virtually all day with the guest ministers they are assigned to. In most cases, they are unable to afford the liberty of the time when they can go and have a 'decent' meal while they are attending to the guest(s).

2. It is normal for most guests to inquire from a protocol officer if he or she has had time to eat. Whereas the rules guiding his or her operation forbids them from seeking for favour from the guest, it is also against the ethics of protocol for members to eat inside the vehicles with which they convey the minister. This is whether the minster is in the vehicle or not, and this is to avoid the distraction that comes from lingering smell of food that would be left inside the car. Perhaps most repelling is the offensive smell of food oozing from the mouth of a protocol personnel after a meal.

3. Even when the guest minster has an hour to refresh and return, the protocol official can hardly afford as much as 20 minutes because they are regularly on the stand by ready to hit the road from the hotel. Given this picture, it is often impossible to have time to go and eat and refresh before the next pick up is due. More often than not, protocol team members forgo their lunch in order to avoid lateness in picking up a guest.

Ideally, the protocol personnel on duty should be accommodated in the same hotel as the guests. It is most times not advisable to allow protocol members on regular schedule to go home late and expect them to return early enough the next morning. Typically, during church programs, protocol officials retire for the day at say 2 am and return to their duty post at say 6 am the same morning.

Apostle Paul wrote: *But by the grace (the unmerited favor and blessing) of God I am what I am, and His grace toward me was not [found to be] for nothing (fruitless and without effect). In fact, I worked harder than all of them [the apostles], though it was not really I, but the grace (the unmerited favor and blessing) of God which was with me*

(1 Corinthians 15:10 (AMP).

4. While on a face value it may appear that the function of the protocol team members portray nothing special yet, it is very peculiar. An involuntary relationship often develops between protocol members and the guest ministers because of their closeness and personalized services they render,

guests often entrust them with their precious personal items such as mobile phones, IPads briefcases, bibles, etc. it is mostly on account of this that protocol officials stay close to the guests so as to allow the guests access to such items whenever they need them. These unpaid image makers for the church therefore, ought to be treated with some extra care.

These reasons explain why it is often not advisable to change protocol frequently in the course of a program. The rule for me at the arrival of guests is to personally introduce the protocol officials to the guests. That is why the integrity, appearance, maturity, sensitivity of the protocol official is of vital importance.

Chapter 6

INFORMATION MANAGEMENT

Information Management

The Protocol Team must believe in strong and effective communication complemented with adequate planning as the key value drivers for achieving excellent service. Even though the central protocol team come together only during major church events, service database is needful.

As a result the following form some core information that must be managed with deft:

a) An up-to-date database of members should be maintained and roster be prepared, updated and communicated timely to team members for clear notification of their roles and responsibilities.

b) The team collaborates with other departments on a need-to-know basis for seamless execution of joint activities. One of such critical departments that are important to the effectiveness of the protocol team is the Ushering department.

c) And most importantly, it is usually expected that members of the protocol department treat all information as confidential. Again the doctrine of need-to-know cannot be over emphasized here.

Without information, it is hardly possible for a protocol team to function optimally.

Information Dissemination

The protocol team members often work under certain unforeseen pressure and this pressure most times is unavoidable. The guests schedule may be changed at short notice. Such that there is hardly enough time for proper adjustments on the part of those keeping watch over them yet, guests have to show up for their engagements.

Clearly such sudden changes are always not convenient but are needful in the overall interest of the ministry organizing the event and therefore developments like these require that protocol members are flexible and proactive. Yet these are persons under authority and must obey authority.

To avoid **complications** of any kind (this is emphasized for planners of church programs to take note), it is not helpful to the interest of everybody to pass valuable instructions or information through too many channels represented by many people.

When an instruction is passed through many channels, in most cases before it gets to the destination, it has become ambiguous and the response that is received may not be exactly what the original message was intended.

The "Pastor Said", **Syndrome**

This statement that is often used to compel people do things without questioning has become an interesting phrase that can mean so many things at different times to different people, depending on the prevailing circumstance.

Noticeably, some people do not have the grace to work under pressure.

Secondly, some leaders do not have the courage to properly double check information and instructions coming from their pastors. Church is not a democracy with checks and balances. So, people say yes most times only to realize later that they have not quite understood the message.

The phrase, 'The Pastor Said…' becomes a handy tool to cover up for mistakes and also to sustain their perceived authority or position of influence. Sometimes, this could be an outright falsehood that has been sent out but because these protocol staff may not have the privilege to directly speak to the pastor, they sheepishly obey instructions that are contrary, thus breeding sometimes frustrations and consequent bad results.

1 Kings 13: 1-19
And, behold, there came a man of God out of Judah by the word of the Lord unto Bethel: and Jeroboam stood by the altar to burn incense.

And he cried against the altar in the word of the LORD, and said, O altar, altar, thus saith the LORD; Behold, a child shall be born unto the house of David, Josiah by name; and upon thee shall he offer the priests of the high places that burn incense upon thee, and men's bones shall be burnt upon thee.

And he gave a sign the same day, saying, This is the sign which the LORD hath spoken; Behold, the altar shall be rent, and the ashes that are upon it shall be poured out.

And it came to pass, when king Jeroboam heard the saying of the man of God, which had cried against the altar in Bethel, that he put forth his hand from the altar, saying, Lay hold on him. And his hand, which he put forth against him, dried up, so that he could not pull it in again to him.

The altar also was rent, and the ashes poured out from the altar, according to the sign which the man of God had given by the word of the LORD.

And the king answered and said unto the man of God, Intreat now the face of the LORD thy God, and pray for me, that my hand may be restored me again. And the man of God besought the LORD, and the king's hand was restored him again, and became as it was before.

And the king said unto the man of God, Come home with me, and refresh thyself, and I will give thee a reward.

And the man of God said unto the king, If thou wilt give me half thine house, I will not go in with thee, neither will I eat bread nor drink water in this place:

For so was it charged me by the word of the LORD, saying, Eat no bread, nor drink water, nor turn again by the same way that thou camest.

So he went another way, and returned not by the way that he came to Bethel.

Now there dwelt an old prophet in Bethel; and his sons came and told him all the works that the man of God had done that day in Bethel: the words which he had spoken unto the king, them they told also to their father.

And their father said unto them, What way went he? For his sons had seen what way the man of God went, which came from Judah.

And he said unto his sons, Saddle me the ass. So they saddled him the ass: and he rode thereon,

And went after the man of God, and found him sitting under an oak: and he said unto him, Art thou the man of God that camest from Judah? And he said, I am.

Then he said unto him, come home with me, and eat bread.

And he said, I may not return with thee, nor go in with thee: neither will I eat bread nor drink water with thee in this place:

For it was said to me by the word of the LORD, Thou shalt eat no bread nor drink water there, nor turn again to go by the way that thou camest.

He said unto him, I am a prophet also as thou art; and an angel spake unto me by the word of the LORD, saying, Bring him back with thee into thine house, that he may eat bread and drink water. But he lied unto him.

So he went back with him, and did eat bread in his house, and drank water.

The reason the prophet went back to the city with the older prophet can be seen in verse 18: *He said unto him, I am a prophet also as thou art; and an angel spake unto me by the word of the LORD, saying, Bring him back with thee into thine house, that he may eat bread and drink water. But he lied unto him.*

Some quick point to note:

> a. I am a prophet also as thou art
>
> b. An angel spake to me by the Lord
>
> c. Bring him back with thee into thine house
>
> d. But he (the older prophet lied) unto him

Verses **23-24**:
And it came to pass, after he had eaten bread, and after he had drunk, that he saddled for him the ass, to wit, for the prophet whom he had brought back. And when he was gone, a lion met him by the way, and slew him: and his carcase was cast in the way, and the ass stood by it, the lion also stood by the carcase.

The consequence of this lie is that the younger prophet died as a result.

You might be wondering and asking the question: do pastors and leaders of today lie in the name of, 'Pastor said…' when the pastor did not say such things? The story of the old prophet and the young one whom he led astray should give us an insight on what dangers there is in this cliché often used to get you to do what ordinarily you may not want to do.

f it happened then and it is written in the scriptures, then yes, they still happen in our day. This is not in any way suggesting that any pastor or leader should be indicted, but we must understand that inferiority complex often hinder people in leadership. Leaders alike could resign to lie so as to maintain their delusion of wielding authority in the eyes of their supposed subordinates.

After all the bibles says,

Now these things befell them by way of a figure [as an example and warning to us]; they were written to admonish and fit us for right action by good instruction, we in whose days the ages have reached their climax (their consummation and concluding period).
- **1 Corinthians 10:11** (AMP)

It is important that instructions and information are free from all forms of ambiguity because the protocol officer or team member who is at the receiving end of this instruction needs this information to render service to every invited guest that the church has planned to show adequate hospitality.

Chapter 7

NEW PHASE

Interestingly due to exigencies of the moment, several other departments now exists to handle other requirements such as hotel accommodation bookings, hospitality arrangements, security, etc. which leaves room for protocol personnel to deal with guest movement, safety and security of personal properties.

In addition, there is the privilege of every member possessing mobile phones and other forms of communication gadgets which makes communications, monitoring and cohesion much easier.

Armour Bearer

This aspect is not directly in line with the context of this mini-book, however certain grey areas need to be removed and completely remove whatever confusion that might have crept in over the years. Especially, with a hanging question whether Armour Bearers are the same as Protocol Officers or are they different, in function and practice. Clearly, the armour bearer is a role founded in the Old Testament practice.

In the Scripture, an armour-bearer was a servant who carried additional weapons for commanders. Some example are Abimelech (**Judges 9:54**), Saul (**1 Samuel**

16:21), Jonathan (**1 Samuel 14:6-17**), and Joab (**2 Samuel 18:15**) they all had armour bearers.

Armour bearers were also responsible for killing enemies wounded by their masters. After enemy soldiers were wounded with javelins or arrows, armour bearers finished the job with clubs or swords. After the time of David, armour bearers were no longer mentioned in the scripture, most likely due to the fact that commanders began to fight from chariots (**1 Kings 12:18; 20:33**).

Some churches today have instituted a figurative position of armour bearer. The duties range widely, but generally speaking, a church armour bearer carries the 'armour' of a church leader, such as the leader's Bible, 'the sword of the Spirit' (**Ephesians 6:17; Hebrews 4:12**). In some instances, a church armour bearer essentially serves as a church leader's bodyguard.

I do not think that the concept of a church armour bearer necessarily contradicts anything in Scripture. Armour bearer or personal assistant may refer to an individual person working with the pastor but protocol may be either individual or a team. I think generally, it is a matter of semantics, what name a church leader chooses to refer to people offering such services. This is dependent on the necessity and what informed the need for such department to be set up.

I therefore presume it is a matter of he who pays the piper, dictates the tune. That is to say, some departments are set up specifically to meet certain needs and their functions are tailored to meet that need. It is dictated and directed by the leader who considered that the department was necessary, after all.

So, not knowing or understanding the purpose for the creation of an armour bearing personnel, may create misinterpretation and misapplication of their functions.

Interestingly, when a protocol person or an armour bearer or personal assistant works with a particular Church leader, a relationship results that goes beyond just what is done in Church. This often extends to the families either way, and boundaries may be crossed or become blurred.

I have seen incorrect use of protocol personnel in Churches where protocol officials are made to serve as personal staff. For instance, they are engaged in things like baby-sitting, personal driver, etc. However, as mentioned earlier, wisdom is profitable to direct.

Some Churches just like many corporate entities, have special security arrangement for their pastors, separate from the general security provided by the Church workers. These people just like the name implies are responsible particularly and primarily for security and safety of the pastor.

The New Testament did not make specific mention of armour bearers and nowhere is it described of any of the apostles, prophets or elders having a person in that role. Likewise, I am not quite sure if there is any specific mention of protocol officer in the bible but, people function today as necessitated by demands of ministries.

Let us have some closer look at some examples of armour bearers and what their functions were.

The Armour Bearer

The armour bearer was a person responsible for the care of a king, officer or other leaders. His job was to refresh, protect and assist his officer.

Elisha

2 Kings 3:13 *But Jehoshaphat asked, 'Is there no prophet of the LORD here that we may inquire of the LORD through him?' An officer of the king of Israel answered, **Elisha,** son of Shaphat is here. He used to pour water on the hands of Elijah. [That is, he was Elijah's personal servant.]*

David

1 Samuel 16:21-23 (AMPC)
And David came to Saul and served him. Saul became very fond of him, and he became his armor-bearer. Saul sent to Jesse, saying, Let David remain in my service, for he pleases me. And when the evil spirit from God was upon Saul, David took a lyre and played it; so Saul was refreshed and became well, and the evil spirit left him.

Barnabas
Acts 4:36-37 (AMPC)
Now Joseph, a Levite and native of Cyprus who was surnamed Barnabas by the apostles, which interpreted

means Son of Encouragement, Sold a field which belonged to him and brought the sum of money and laid it at the feet of the apostles.

Useful principles necessary to possess the attitudes of a God-appointed assistant

Be a gracious representative. Know that in your serving, you are representing God and your officer. If you have to defer someone to protect your leader's time, (as in the example given above), be gracious. You can be gentle but firm with God's sheep

Recognize God still calls and appoints leaders and assistants today. Remember our Lord Jesus is the same, yesterday, today and forever.

As an armour bearer, you are a God-appointed assistant called to support the man or woman of God. Begin to look at your assistantship as a ministry unto the Lord.

An Armour bearer or personal assistant to the senior pastor should have a strong desire to assist the Pastor, ministry leaders, and ministry guests. There is a reason God gave us spiritual gifts and talents to equip us for ministry.

You will be expected to redeem or enhance your leader's time. In the book of Acts, Stephen and Phillip were among the seven assigned to take care of the details of ministry while the Apostles ministered before the Lord.

You have to learn to discern your leader's spirit. Sometimes, your officer is operating in their God-ordained office under the anointing and at other times, they are just being themselves.

Respect them, either way. When it is time to relax with your leader, be a good friend and relax but when it is time to take care of the Father's business and His people, slip back into the working mode with them.

Guard against familiarity. Familiarity will affect how others look at your leader. If you are being too familiar at inappropriate times, it will cause respect for your leader to drain. Remain respectful of his authority.

Be one of their strongest allies. Show that you are always for them. In words and action, support their authority. If you discover criticism in others, work to show the good side of your leader's heart.

Duties of an Armour Bearer

- To have a deep-down sense of respect for the leader, and acceptance for and tolerance for the leaders' personality and their way of doing things.

- To provide strength to the leader

- To exalt and uplift the leader

- You must instinctively understand the leader's thoughts

- Must be able to repel any kind of attack against his or her leader, especially have the leader's back

- Keeps watch while the leader rests (**1 Sam. 17:55-58; 1 Sam. 26:5-7,14-16**)

- Cares for his belongings

- Reacts with total intolerance to any false accusations against the leader (rumours, gossip, talking behind his back, etc.)

- Demonstrate extreme loyalty

Advent of the PSA

Church growth comes with its peculiar requirements and it is for this reason that each ministry is encouraged to evolve the best way to manage security and ensure that the relationship between the Pastors and the congregation is best coordinated in an orderly manner.

Whenever the work of God begins to spread it is also the appropriate time to ensure efficient management of people and conducts because such times are when people visits the church from different quarters to see what the Lord is doing in the church.

The Bible says in Matthew 24:28,
"For wheresoever the carcase is, there will the eagles be gathered together".

At such times of church growth is also a time to put in place control of access to the pastor and guest ministers to the church's programs hence, the need to create specialized departments or sub-units for this purpose.

For this purpose of this discourse, one unit that became imperative in my experience was what became known as the Pastors Security Aid department (PSA). The role of this department was primarily "to protect and provide security for the pastor and the ministers that come to the church".

Whilst the Protocol department provided assistance for the Pastor and Ministering guests, the Pastor's Aid provided security directly for their person. Controlled access to most servants of God is necessitated by the overwhelming distractions from people in the form of conversations and issues that are capable of hindering the pastor's effectiveness.

Imagine these two scenarios:

1. An influential neighbour with a claim that the church was disturbing his peace confronts the Pastor at the gate of the church as he was getting ready for the day's ministration. This neighbor bombards him with disturbing words capable of upsetting his mind. The Protocol officer could not do much since he is carrying the Pastor's belongings. Hence, the PSA officer became necessary to prevent such a person from planting a word of distraction in him.

2. Imagine this other scenario where the Pastor is getting to church and making his way to the front to take his seat, gather his thoughts before being ushered to the pulpit to minister the word of God. And a member of the congregation approaches the Pastor with a complaint of how a standing usher maltreated them in church.

In every organization or setting, there are protocols guiding everything. For instance, an individual cannot just walk up to the President of a country, a King or Chief Executive Officer of an organization whenever you want to. There are protocols built around such persons and they must be observed. If you break protocol, it could have dire consequences. These are men or women in society whose office cannot afford the luxury of cheap talk with their time. The man or woman of God who is on assignment for the Lord is no less important. **1 Cor. 14:40** says,

Let all things be done decently and in order.

One other reason for the establishment of this service to the man of God or the ministers of God is to dissuade familiarity that leads to breach in protocol. There are people who by virtue of prior knowledge or acquaintances with the pastor and or a minister, believe they should have un-restricted access to them. This ought not to be so. The pastor or minister may seem available physically, yet he might be meditating on something concerning his message and should not be disturbed. It is also possible that the Lord is dealing with him/her at that particular point in time. Allowing access to them at that time could constitute a distraction. The pastor or minister may just want to be left alone to work through these things with little or no distraction.

In **Esther 4:11 & 5:1-2**, we see a very interesting situation.

Esther 4:11

All the king's servants, and the people of the king's provinces, do know, that whosoever, whether man or women, shall come unto the king into the inner court, who is not called, there is one law of his to put him to death, except such to whom the king shall hold out the golden sceptre, that he may live: but I have not been called to come in unto the king these thirty days.

Esther 5:1-2

Now it came to pass on the third day that Esther put on her royal apparel, and stood in the inner court of the king's house, over against the king's house: and the king sat upon his royal throne in the royal house, over against the gate of the house.
And it was so, when the king saw Esther the queen standing in the court, that she obtained favour in his sight: and the king held out to Esther the golden sceptre that was in his hand. So Esther drew near, and touched the top of the sceptre.

From the above scripture, we can see that there must have been someone on hand to prevent people from getting into the king's presence without invitation.

There are also instances where access should be denied strictly for security purposes such as prevent someone with a wrong motive (or evil intention) from getting to the Pastor. There is no reason why the church should always be 'reactive'. It ought to be 'proactive' and not have to learn from after the fact.

Requirements

The Pastor's Security Aid like the Protocol officer must be one given to prayer and sensitive to the Holy Spirit. As with every work in the church setting, we must allow the Holy Spirit to help and guide our operations at all times. This is a key element to success in ministry at whatever position we find ourselves. The words of Jesus in **John 15:5** rings out loudly:

I am the vine, ye are the branches: He that abideth in me, and I in him, the same bringeth forth much fruit: for without me ye can do nothing.

The aforementioned instances are typical regular occurrences in churches across the world. Having trained personnel to provide these services have become expedient. A protocol officer who is carrying the belongings of the pastor or minister will have a hard time shielding him or her from unwarranted contacts. It is therefore expedient to have another person play that role. In many cases, it may be required for more than one person to play such a role (especially in a crowded environment where everyone wants to touch the pastor).

Unknown to most people, most Pastors do not like to engage in any conversation before they enter the pulpit to minister. The presence of an assistant or aid can help manage these circumstances.

POSTSCRIPT

To most people, serving God appears to be an effort in futility. After all, it is easy to point one or more persons who have served God for as long as they can remember but, there is so little or nothing to show for it. However, it must be borne in mind that God rewards those who 'diligently' serves Him. It invariably means that there is an assured reward awaiting the man or woman who remains consistent and unwavering in serving God.

In this context, there is a place for patience, persistence, courage before we can receive after we have done what is required of us as Christians.

Unfortunately, in certain cases, a man may be doing all that he or she can in order to just get God to do what he or she wants. Turning God into a tool that you can use for your selfish gain is not the same thing as serving God in truth and in spirit.

We must learn to turn from self-seeking and instead, seek the things of God. According to **Luke 9:23-24**, *And He said to them all, if any man will come after me, let him deny himself, and take up his cross daily, and follow me. For whosoever will save his life shall lose it, but whosoever will lose his life for my sake, the same shall save it.*

What is it that we have that was not given to us by God? Peter makes it clear that we have received our gifts from God. Serving is not about us receiving attention or glory; it s for God alone to receive glory. Giving God all the glory will cause people to examine and be drawn into the life-changing nature of a relationship with Jesus Christ. And even much more, it will validate our faith before non-Christians.

As we are drawn into His life changing nature, we are also to grow in obedience of Christ and love for his people. Nothing works outside of love with our God hence, we are encouraged to serve Him in love and let this love that has been shed abroad in our hearts be made manifest in everything that we do.

We must ensure that we have a growing knowledge of love for God's truth as revealed in His word (**1John 2:21-27**).

However, in order to walk in the fullness of God's plan and purpose for our lives and work the work that He has commended unto us, we are to seek Him at all times, Each man or woman that is called to serve in the Lord's vineyard, must as a matter of priority practice a quiet time alone with the Lord.

This time alone with God is absolutely your responsibility. And whenever the opportunity to be alone with Him is presented, utilise such times to engage in prayer and communicate with God.

It is almost impossible for anyone called into Protocol service to go far without seeking the Lord with diligence through prayers, meditation and all manner of communication with Him. Doing otherwise will only lead such a person into the sin of Gehazi as we saw earlier. The moment any servant of the Lord takes his or her attention off the Lord, Satan cause such an individual to put focus on himself or herself. Then you begin to hear statements like, 'I did all this myself', or as the world often say, 'I am a self-made man or self-made woman.' We can do nothing ourselves except what the Lord has given us the grace to achieve.

It is for this reason that Matthew 6:33 (*But seek ye first the kingdom of God, and His righteousness, and all these things shall be added unto you*), becomes an imperative for a child of God who intends to serve Him unto all pleasing. Ironically, more often than not, persons who get frustrated and stray away from the Lord, are quite closer than they could image, of entering into God's rest when they quit.

That is the reason we need to mix our faith with patience and perseverance, among other fruits of the spirit. As far as serving the Lord diligently is concerned, everything that we do must be mixed with faith. **Hebrew 4:2**, *For unto us was the gospel preached, as well as unto them: but the word preached did not profit them, not being mixed with faith in them that heard it.*

Who is the Best Protocol Official?

This appears to be the million dollar question that every man or woman called into service as protocol official in any ministry must seek to answer. Indeed, it is an aspiration that must be pursued with all diligence. Having done all hat is required of you, you must remain standing until the very end.

n my description of the Elijah – Elisha model which was my guide towards becoming a successful protocol official; he one thing that played out till the very end in the relationship between the master and his servant, is that Elisha stood until the end.

Even when the master Elijah made efforts to dissuade him (another way of saying that your faith will be put to the test n the course of the journey), Elisha was desirous of the double portion and the only way that could happen is if he could stay with his master until the very end. He stayed out the time. Was it an easy task? Obviously, it could not have been an easy task.

2 Kings 2:1-15, paints a vivid picture of all that happened on the last part of Elijah's journey here on earth. See **verses 9 – 12**:
And it came to pass, when they were gone over, that Elijah said unto Elisha, Ask what I should do for thee, before I be taken away from thee. And Elisha said, I pray thee, let a double portion of thy spirit be upon me.
And he said, thou hast asked a hard thing: nevertheless, if thou see me when I am taken from thee, it shall be so unto thee, but if not, it shall not be so.
And it came to pass, as they still went on, and talked, that, behold there appeared a chariot of fire, and horses of fire, and parted them both asunder, and Elijah went up by a whirlwind into heaven.

And Elisha saw it, and he cried, My father, my father, the chariot of Israel, and the horsemen thereof, and he saw him no more...

What happened after the episode narrated above was that Elisha obtained everything that he asked of his master by simple act of patience and tenacious waiting, till the end.

Often, the man or woman who qualifies in the eyes of man as the best Protocol official is that person who has the best physiological attributes – tall, well built and appears well dressed at all times. Yes, indeed these attributes are good but the best Protocol official is that person who is able to last until the very end doing what God has called him or her to do come rain or sunshine.

It is better to remain committed until the last day of your assignment. And if the Lord tarries, that you maintain such credible record until the day you are called unto the next higher assignment. Next higher assignment? Yes, I know by experience and by observing the ways of the Lord, that you can hardly finish your course remaining on the same spot.

And the reward for hard and productive work is more work, I dare say more glorious works. What is it that is written about the path of the righteous? The Psalmist says it is like the dawn of anew day which shines brighter and brighter unto the perfect day.

This is the only true testimony that awaits the man or woman who qualifies as the best protocol team member.

Generations after generations, changes in times and tides, size and nomenclature, all put together cannot alter the function of a true servant of the Lord who is called to duty as a protocol official.

This aspiration is desirous to those who are completely sold out for the LORD!

I wish you Godspeed in the journey that you have embarked on.